HOW IT SHONE

HOW IT SHONE

KATHERINE BARHAM

atmosphere press

Table of Contents

To Katy

Those Cows at "The Roost"

Below the bedroom window, mornings
you could hear them munching. Nights
they would lie in the dark, their backs to us,

huge convalescent lumps, breathing on the fields.
In the dream I am running, a suitcase
bumping each hip, a ticket to the future

fluttering from my mouth. I'm boarding the train
when I turn to face whole herds of Holsteins,
gazing. "Come back,"

their eyes implore, and the dream ends.
They resume the long walk back to the barn
without me, as well they should.

While built for birth and giving milk,
they are not particularly kind; attachment
unsettles them. Beyond bearing witness

they can't commit to much. Evenings
they must still stroll to the barbed-wire fence,
stand by the pine with the yellow jackets' nest

and stare and chew. When they walk
their bodies make a swishing sound,
each step deliberate as one freight
car knocking another.

The Drive Back to Virginia

So many silos still
along Interstate 81,
a few barns, the token
rusted tin roof, a hint of cow manure,
some calves who lounge below a stand of trees,
all undeterred by prefabs
and telephone towers.
My own nostalgia withstands the roar
and aftershock of semis, the Kelly green
and yellow Luray Caverns billboard
blaring "Acres of Nature." Cheesy
but so is today's crushed velvet
of the Blue Ridge Mountains. Autumn is gaudy.
For example, that glint
off Walmart's fleet of sleeping trucks.

Dialogue With a Bull in a Large
Framed Photograph

The first time I saw your photograph
mounted above the landlady's blue vase
of dust-laden plastic hyacinths,
I thought you were funny. A solid engine
of flesh on little stubs for legs
wading in spring's glittering hay,
staring dully ahead, oblivious to
freshly brushed fur, the neat braid
gracing your thick withers, the ostentatious
titles over your head—Prince Eric Esquire Grand
Champion—
overkill, if you will.

Last summer I sat in a bar
in San Sebastian where pitchers of sangria
glowed blood red and bullfights blared
on the television. "No contest!" I gestured
at the bartender after three bulls were dragged
across the dusty, raucous arena.
He shook his head and lifted
his shirt, baring the justification:
across his middle a long purple scar.

Sonnet to a Drowned Groundhog

All winter long it had lain among algae and leaves,
its gaze skyward.
What drove it, I wonder, from the hole in the field
to the hole in the water?
Perhaps one spring day charged with possibility,
it lumbered, fur riffling, across the Burtons' pasture,
found our chain-link fence, burrowed under
and plunged, on principle, from the familiar.

Immutable now, it takes up half the pool,
a disfigured behemoth, but I make it benign,
a witness bearer
to that day my cousins and I tread water,
the way 45 minutes later, the medal,
a foil-wrapped quarter etched FROG, glitters.

Richmond August Dusk

The air is haywire with cicadas
who sing the city's trees to stumps,
the women who planted them to ash.

The moon, a flung fingernail,
has nothing to say.

Summer Ride

Driving home late
a spray of moths in the headlights
spots of singing from the woods

August air thick as the buttermilk halo
around tonight's moon
a crescent riding her curve

contagious as the word *raccoon*
wind effacing thought
into the dark

no one else on the road
something gnawing
the red flash of an animal's eyes

then the fox darts out
and runs before my brights
slowing down I watch it gain

on the moons of my headlights—
guiding me home.

Blessed

Here in the quiet twilight
a floral family surrounds me:

92-year old Rita Williams' antique roses
which began as a rooted cutting
from fresh cut flowers 20 years ago,
my landlady tells me.

The tiger lily whose eight stems
began as one,
Vinca
Clematis
Elephant Ear
Jewelweed
Jewels of Opar, whose pods
resemble tiny rubies
Verbena Bonariensis
Latinate and lovely
purple clusters—
all here years before I was.

Sitting among them, I recall
Confirmation classes and first communion,
The Laying on of Hands.

The moonflower blossom is cupped
and white as the Virgin Mother
and holy.

July 4th, 2012

In the sizzle of fireworks
and hundred-degree heat,
we retreat to the house, still
without power, my parents
in their eighties, still
stoical, helping haul water bottles
in from the garage.

I remembered watching some bumblebees
who drank for days on end
from the butterfly bush,
their wings folded
primly against their backs,
no gaudy gold show,
no loudmouth buzzing.
Those bees meant business.
In unison they sucked, heads down,
from bloom to bloom
in hunger or in ceremony.

Unseason

Longings
spin gravel and go, leaving me
quiet as a shrub in autumn light.
This must be the season
when empty beach motels
speak to the ocean,
when summer clothes rest in cedar closets,
and hearts wear neon VACANCY signs.

Alone but Happy When the First Snow Falls

You wake to the singular scrape of a shovel
and silence of snow that has fallen on itself
all night long.
Heaped up to the window ledge
and over the yard
before a child builds a snowman
or a dog rolls in it for the first time,
it remains a secret
between you and those sparrows
conspiring from the telephone wire.

Snowstorm

Instead of making soup or digging
the car out of the driveway, I'd like
to be curled in sleep like the cat
or smoke—

still as a moth waiting on a wall
or black cow on a white field—
while the blizzard of the century
makes the pine boughs droop,

the birdfeeder sway
and the finches fight for food.
Waiting for the lights to go out,
I imagine exile: living like the broom sage

there below the flat sky
some birds darken.

Against Anthropomorphics

The amaryllis blooms belie the stalks' surrender.
Yesterday I staked the spires bent from leaning
toward the light, and today's red bursts
proclaim ambition. Truth be told, these naked ladies
don't mock my January lethargy.

They do what they do—
as the baby blue jay who hits the windowpane,
flits and finding no roost,
lands on the lower roof,
or the bat trapped in my Auroville guest house bathroom,
who keeps orbiting
or the starving dog I fed
who keeps returning to the Solar Kitchen parking lot—

all not knowing what they know
nor needing to.

I, Phalorope

Less girly than some shorebirds' names
with a hint of myth. And not to brag
but my red plumage puts my mate's to shame.
While he stays with our young, I gallivant
in salty waters, buoyant.
At mealtime when I whirl and spin,
prey caught,
I rise from the depths, and I dine.

No nesting instinct here
no need for domesticity's
long slow stir
those sips you lift daintily
from a spoon.

Blood Moon

This pairing carries clout, a hint of treachery,
but it's not me. Even at my most luminescent
I am wan beside the others, an outcast among
the constellations—even when—especially when—
full, but the fact that scientists,
not poets, keep this coinage
is endearing. Everyone loves a lunar eclipse,
but isn't the main draw my diminishing?
At best I leave a blush behind,
and the distance between *blood* and *blush*
vast as that from sky to earth.

But for those of you below
who rose from sleep on my behalf,
I will honor your moniker, apt or not.
Besides, your planet plays a part
in this display of color, along with that day star
that takes its light for granted. Were it not for all its rises
and falls, the bending of its light,
I would simply disappear into the dark,
return to anonymity—be, in your terms,
blood*less.* Drained.
Be, in mine, *pearled.*

Spring Sabbatical

The commerce in the trees
reiterates my leisure.
Even the bumblebees rush,
orbiting, as if to land meant stasis.
I languish a little longer, conspire
to aristocracy, to own the road
at 10 a.m. Thwarted by traffic and leisure
of the *permanently* retired, the smack of fact—
I'm geriatric, too, but bound for work next year—
I head for home, loll on the porch,
ensconced in wicker.
Below me, the bullfrog, would-be
double bassist, sounds a single note,
a complicit twang.

Retiring

The earth is a handful of signs
to today's array: a singular note from a jay
songbird chatter   varied voices
insistent as summer's heat
and slow
as that river of molasses taffy
that flowed from the sideboard shelf
onto the floor
that river of my grandmother's laughter

Cracking Brazil Nuts

This one's a petrified
elephant ear before I split
it. A faint dirt smell.
See the ridged, prehistoric
spine on the next one.
Deformities.
Woody and hairless
with secrets to guard.
The goal is to crack it just so
the whole nut falls.

My plate's become
a demolition site
a paleontology gone wrong
The last one won't
be cracked.
Imagine it lying in a forest
forever, a moon inside,
an egg that won't hatch.

Incipience

When the leaves skitter
across the roof when the squirrels skitter
across the road to score more acorns
accounting for the tiny thud
when one drops from a branch
to the ground
when secret creatures skitter
in roadside foliage
when the very air skitters
with light when you arrive home
when you don't know where to skitter
next so you stand in the silence
when the hoarse cries of the geese
have stopped when the silent
photo of your father stands
static and startling
as the past's taxidermy.

Chinquapin

This morning I swerved
and just missed one squirrel
chasing another across the road
when the word darted into my thoughts
in the same staccato
it sprang from my father's lips
that day on our walk.

Chinky-pin is how he said it
when we stood among fields
and electrical hum of insects
somewhere between the end of our lane
and Riner Thompson's farm.

While his hands worked the prickly hull
away from the small globe,
I leaned against my walking stick
which continued to sweat
an hour after he carved it.

A Eulogy for Robert T. Barham

To look at anything—
You must be the thing you see.
　　　　--James Moffett

My father bore witness to the things of this world,
but he wouldn't presume to be them.
He seemed to form alliances with birds—once a bob-white
whistled back—
and persimmons, mountain laurels, chinquapin bushes.

And he needed to know the names of things.
As a child I grew tired of his botanical litanies,
but "You there tree, fruit, leaf or fern"
would not do.

He held a reverence
for rituals, too. Walks required walking sticks—
carved ones, no less—and cooking oatmeal
every morning became a solemn enactment.

The last time he came to visit,
I took him to Reading Terminal Market,
where he insisted on buying a fish (a halibut)
to take, smelling to high heaven, on the train

to cook for our dinner.
The preparation was elaborate: a profusion of spices,
commentary on the importance of garlic
and seasoning salt and high heat—
and the finished fish far too bony to eat.

Vigil

Mama Robin has been on her nest on the rafter
for days, still as a stone, impossibly patient.
I worry that she doesn't eat,
wonder who provides *her*

with nourishment. I hope the bird facing her
I saw at dusk was her mate with food in his beak.
I just read that she leaves the nest in the morning
for five to ten minutes

to feed on earthworms so her body
can handle the demands
of laying an egg.
Not to mention incubation!

Once hatched the nestlings get fed
by both parents up to 40 times a day.
Such rigorous parenting!
I have no children nor mate

but my dachscund, who died 34 days ago,
feels like a daughter lost
even though she was old (10) when I got her.
Still, the space beside me

where she slept
and where she died
hasn't shrunk
and the hours I fed her
stay irrelevant

and the food that drops to the floor
stays untouched
and the house when I return
stays empty,   echoey.

Mother Love

When my cat perched upside down from the bluebird
house
    and peered down into the opening,
the mother bird, out of nowhere
                swooped down and brushed
his back with her wings.

    I recalled that spring night
my mother, cloaked in her black lace mantilla,
greeted me at the door—my sisters in tow—
and bore us to the Colony House Motel
because a bat was in the house.

My sisters and I, blasé about the bat,
reveled in spending a school night in a motel
        and having pecan waffles at the Toddle House
before school the next day. It turned out the bat
had gotten out of the house

and the exterminator had come for naught.
Of course the cat could not have entered the bluebird
house, anyway.
It turned out the baby bluebirds were oblivious
as my sisters and I to inherent harm. It turns out that my
mother, young and glamorous,
the envy of all my friends,

        now in her eighties, lies with her
head in my lap (nested)
chin raised, exposing whiskers she asks and trusts me to
tweeze.

        I brush my wings across her face.
This is a poem, not a news report.

March Snowstorm

While the blizzard of the century
made the pine trees droop

and the birdfeeder sway,
we played long games of scrabble,

drank bourbon, dug out candles
and waited for the power

to go out. The second day
more of the same, the lights

still on, the jars full of water
still untouched and glazed

as the cars we took brooms and shovels
to when the novelty of being snowed

in wore off and the men we said
we needed had not

shown.
While the white wind

blew the snow we swept
back and tires whirred in their ruts,

I recalled the insistent way
the house finches had fought the air

and each other for food
and found myself pushing harder

while you manned the steering wheel.
On the third try,

when we rocked the first car
out, the only sounds

were the snow's hollow crunch
and wingbeats.

Brief Instructions for Retrieving the Past

A crunch of wheels outside. Running into the house,
still wearing her coat, my grandmother,
no longer dead, briskly unties one of the rugs
rolled and bound on the floor
and tells me to stand at one fringed end
and slide the length of it. It is my favorite,
the *Tree of Life*, the green, gold and red
Oriental. "Impossible," I say,
but she lifts the sleeves of her coat,
spreading like branches, plants her feet together
and flies right up to the tree's lush crown.
"No way," I repeat.
Then, as if by
accident, I glide. What loud brilliant birds!
What silent little eggs.

March Madness

I am the naysayer,
the narcoleptic in the stands
still hung over from springing
forward. Immune
to the commerce in the trees,
outburst of forsythia
and rush of bumblebees,

I lumber along, recall
falling back and its sanction to sleep.
I am a she-bear, unaware,
still dozing,
an earthworm,
exposed, recalling
the cool subterranean,

the rooty odor of exile.
I am Eve, *pre*-Paradise
until recess is over
and droves of seventh graders, oxide-scented,
stampede in, boys slap-boxing boys,
girls cavorting in short shorts.

Bus Duty

Adolescent boys linger beside sleek
pickup trucks before school starts.
When I ask them to move onto the sidewalk,
no one budges. One kicks gravel
with his boot. Another slap-boxes his slouching
friend. One whose hands are thrust in his pockets
looks through me. Invisible.
The space around their wheels is charmed
with entitlement. Soon though,
the tardy bell will ring and tear them away
from their dream of becoming
or riding nowhere in particular, loudly.

Oil Change

"Oil is the blood of the car," a man I used to date,
admonished when I failed to check or change my oil.

Today I sit on the overstuffed vinyl couch
at Clark's Automotive, grading essays, awaiting my oil
change. Once I learned they were open Saturdays,
 I vowed to come every 3000 miles.
I know these guys by name.
Archie runs the place and delegates; Willis does the work
on my 2004 Subaru, and it's rare I get out
with an oil change alone. Like surgeons
Willis or Archie will emerge from the garage, bearing a
faulty part,
as if I recognized its name, much less the malady. I
wouldn't know
a damaged axle seal if it bit me, but nod as if I did,
as if they had my car's and my own best interest at heart.
Truth be told, I envy these men their ease in this domain
of grease and metal,
the patina of their tools and trade,
their messy, sexy lexicon:

throttle body
manifold
right rear axle seal
harmonic balancer
rear rotors
caliper slides
front struts

January Ode to Clarence

Tonight, listening to the rain's
papery monosyllables on the window,
I know there are words I can turn to—
but Clarence, you appear
instead, hunched and overalled,
walking Riner's dusty hills,
disappearing occasionally in the curve
of the road. I imagine
the two of us riding in the back
of Riner Thompson's hay truck
over buxom fields in summer.
You paw at my arm and smile shyly.
You cannot talk (or won't)
but stories flow from your eyes,
deer-bright.

At Daybreak

Barely discernible in the half-dark
and stone still where the field forms a *V*
down near the tree line, five of them,
a family, no doubt, lie with their backs
to me. It's rare to see deer lying down
this close to the house, this nonchalant.
Rare, too, that I rise this early
and walk to the window.

They are oblivious to me; it's good
they don't know I imagine joining them,
especially that doe who rises,
walks to a branch and lifts her throat.

The Wedding Reception

While the band takes a break,
guests lounge on the Boar's Head patio,
a fleet of wrought-iron tables,
flagstone and white. One swan,
anchored to the pond below,
keeps his head erect and gaze aloof as my own.
A few Canada geese, all legs and pose,
preen on shore.

My first Floyd Ward Ballroom dance
Girl's Choice undid me.
The swan is out of the water now
snatching something from the bank,
oblivious to the mass of flailing arms in the lit
ballroom, those geese gliding back
across the pond into themselves.

Intimation

The maple in the yard still
has leaves peroxide-brown.

Another one drops, startling
the cats at play.

Late November is undressing
its last tree. In the sky

a woman with worn hands
clutches her gray shawl close,

recalling a bouffant hairdo
and sapphire-blue gown

that rustled when she walked.

This Friday Night

I am moored to the couch,
empty as a stilled drum.
If I need anything
it must only be air.
If there are thoughts in my head
they float idly by.
If I had to define what I am not doing,
it must be having a shirtwaist hemmed:

Standing still as a post
till I must turn just so,
my mother sitting on the floor below,
yardstick in hand, straight pins in mouth,
muffling a threat to begin again.

Notes Taken From the Laundromat

Sunday afternoon. February air
thick outside.
The medley of buttons tapping dryer walls
and thwacks from the machine spitting
quarters are wordier than our faces.
My hand pours in the soap.
I stand over my clothes, eyeing
the matted clumps of Blue Cheer,
the quills of water rushing in—
until my mound of sweaters after the rinse cycle
becomes the dead groundhog floating in the pool
twenty-five years ago—totem
for the winter-bloated day.

Filigree

Seeing her backlit like that
almost seems illicit. The caught beetle,
recalcitrant and twice her size,
her web, the largest I have seen,
a grid of filaments
that shimmer on the window screen.

And then dismantled.
In the morning no such suspension
though a leaf shard hangs
and from the porch a glint of cable
stretches toward a tree.

In the corners of the house
more transfigurations:
mosquito leg
moth wing

Process

While bright stuffed mice and toys with bells inside
gather dust under the couch, my cat
bats another half-alive mouse
around the deck. Quivering
carnage, small entrails by the door, heads
left open-eyed horrified me.
Feathers were the worst, especially downy
ones. I'd look the other way and wish
he wouldn't linger over his kill.
Sometimes I'd pry the victims loose.

Lately, I watch his precision,
not the blood or crack
of bone. His body, utterly still,
tenses before the catch. No wonder
he can't contain himself once the mouse is in his
jaws. Then the real work starts:
tossing the body in the air,
nudging it gently when it lands,
running sideways,
the culminating vocals.
The best endings are clean,
when everything's used.

Just the cat, washing.

Varieties of Helplessness

I.

More important than losing
all my teeth at once
is keeping it secret.
I'm conversing with someone
at a party when one by one
my teeth fall out.
Painless extractions these
but saving face, as it were,
exhausting. I'm mid-
sentence when it happens,
so my mouth clamps shut
and all talking stops.
The dream does not end there, though.
Since not being found out
means more than losing my teeth,
I'm strategizing how to pick
up where I left off without
my teeth spilling out
onto the floor.
Even if they did and the other person
chose to ignore it, surely my words
would turn to mush,
socially unacceptable as sudden
silence.

2.

"Don't scream, I've got a gun,"
the man who had followed me to the restroom,
said. He spoke barely above a whisper,
but it stunned me silent,

at least until I saw his car, a black charger (what else)?
at the far end of the country store parking lot
pointed toward the highway.
By this time I reasoned that being shot
would be better than getting into that car,
that if he had a gun, wouldn't I feel it pressed
against my back? And with that, I screamed. He bolted
for his car and I bolted for my caramel-colored Gremlin
and raced out of the parking lot,
despite the large number of people outside the store
who had heard me scream. More worried about being late
to the Moody Blues concert than my previous peril,
I sped down the highway.
We arrived to Justin Hayward's crooning, "Nights
in White Satin." (What else)?

Ideal Woman

Daphne, huntress once, and fleet of foot,
is now root. Thanks to Peneus' spell,
she's all tree, Apollo's second fantasy,
(his first to have her in his bed,
then, as a wreath upon his head
and other victors' too)!
Static and inanimate, she'll make a truer
mate, now that leaf and branch supplant

a brain; and feet
in subterranean state remain.
She'll stay more loyal as a laurel
than as a *she*.
Sun, wind or rain her only quarrel,
mute as a stone as Apollo's tree.

Stinkbug
Leptoglossus occidentalis

The article says if you let them walk on you,
they won't hurt you, but if you hold one in your hand,
it will stab you with its beak.

Last week one of these vilified, shield-shaped
but not noble, plodding, dogged
creatures lay in my bathroom windowsill.

Just the night before, winged,
it had flown around the room enticing the cats.
Now I study its carcass encased in toilet paper,

remembering the way it waved
its four and a half legs, shield side down,
and how I tried to tip it upright with a pencil,

careful not to trigger any stink. Each time
it chose to be prone, wearied perhaps
from its trip from the porch to the bathroom

or recent amputations. I pondered
euthanasia but walked away, checking it
each day, giving it up for dead,

but upon tapping it,
a leg or antenna would wave
almost cordially.

On the fourth day it lay still
at my pencil's prodding,
legs folded primly across its abdomen,

antennae bent backward.
Last month, arriving home from work,
I found my porch missing a wall,

the landlady's excuse, "The carpenter
just showed up!" Four weeks later
I stand in the kitchen doorway:

out on the porch, my desk upended,
furniture shrouded,
stench of caulk.

Hairbrush

The hairbrush was large, made of hard clear plastic.
Add to that bristles that beat down on my bare butt

laying red welts
like scouring but quicker.

"She had it coming," Fran, my mother's friend
in Birmingham, might have said afterwards.

Truth be told I deserved punishment
for tossing rocks at Becky Cantrell

simply sitting on her porch on a summer day.
I don't know what got into me

while riding my blue bicycle,
nor where I got the rocks, which I remember as gravel,

but I prefer to think I was testing my aim
more than malice. (Note that I said *tossing*, not *pelting*).

As far as I know, Becky had done me no harm.
Goody-goody. Pale skin

and light red hair, timid.
I've witnessed sudden savagery in other children, too

but that hairbrush from my mother's hand
that bore my mother's embarrassment

more savage than my crime deserved.
Hairbrush. Spondaic. Heavy.

Unlike the sound of *brush*
or that bird's wings brushing the air
with absolution.

One Summer

I saw June Thompson chop off a chicken's head
and the body defiantly hop around.
Then her husband Riner took a ping-pong paddle
to the baby starlings in his barn's eaves.

          I couldn't stop dwelling
on the loud whacks and waiting
for the peeps to stop, the way
he tossed the bodies in the nest
               like twigs, lowered the ladder
and left, to check the cows, maybe,
without a word.

              I suppose ridding
barn eaves of birds was part of Riner's business.

              I suppose my sister
forgave me when I whacked the baseball
into her eye, broke her nose and gave her a shiner

that changed colors.
Her small face took forever to fade.

A Winter Reunion

You spoke the words slowly, voice low, slightly guttural:
"Your eyes sometimes turn watery and dark."

We were huddled over coffees in the booth
at the back of a dark café, while January's

refusals gathered outside. Instead of saying,
"Only when I'm lonely or sad" or "Is loving you

a phenomenon?" I thought of San Francisco's
Seal Rock. Last November I scanned the bay

for any sleek bobbing head to emerge
or cries from their stony haven.

No sign of them. Then, something sudden and black—
an arm, perhaps, or tossing, sun-washed head—

flashed from a high rock,

inviting me now, to slide
from the booth's slick seat

into stupefying cold—
and glide beyond confusion, speech.

Valentine's Snow Day

I've nursed this fire for hours—
as if my life depended on it
or the heat weren't cranked up
or you who taught me how to build fires
didn't dump me last year
or that the rising flames
resembling wings or one rearranged
log and each ember tended
to resurrect a feeble flame
mattered—as if
the silence of snow falling on itself
drowned out the edicts of ice
and the demolition next door—as if
a promise glowed.

Clarence Poem 2

I wonder what happened to Clarence, the man in
bibbed overalls, young but slightly stooped, we always saw
walking the dusty Riner roads in summer. My
grandmother would stop and offer him rides. The two of
us sat on the scratchy back seat of her green Packard,
hugging our windows, silence growing between us.
Rumor had it that Clarence was "mute," so I didn't try to
talk to him. I was nine or ten, and Clarence probably in
his twenties. He had older brothers who my grandmother
said were up to no good. Clarence looked like an angel,
though, with deer-bright eyes that stared ahead.

Turns out Clarence was one of Riner Thompson's farm
hands, and once he was riding on the hay truck with me
and Sara Jane, Riner's daughter, and some other men who
must have been farm hands, too. The air was sticky with
insects. I can't tell you what happened before Clarence
patted my arm, or why he did it, but I took it as friendly.
What happened next was everyone, including Sara Jane,
started laughing. I didn't understand why, and I assume
Clarence didn't either. Soon there were taunts like
"Kathy's got a boyfriend" and more laughing. I wish I
could remember what happened next. I wish I could say I
stood up for Clarence or stood mute beside him. I wish
when I conjure him he weren't always walking away.

Snake Story

At least twenty shots
range from the rifle you fired, close range
at the black snake, our cellar dweller

I'd named Joe the summer I was ten. He'd
stopped the mice nesting in the pink brocade chair.
You were the youngest mother

on the block, a glittering bracelet
I flaunted at the kindergarten kids
on the train ride to Garden City.

The hairdresser swore we were sisters
and called you glamorous.
"All that glitters is not gold"

was my father's retort to his friend
who had said, "Your wife is gorgeous."
When I was fourteen he announced he was leaving.

After you shot the snake, you pelted it with rocks.
What I remember most
is the time it took the snake to die,

how it shone, writhing
magnificently in the dust.

The Roost's Men

Though dead since my mother was thirteen, my grandfather
Carl remained in the house,
insistent as the moose head's glass gaze.
The story went that one of Carl's friends had shot the moose
whose head my mother and her sisters dubbed Oscar. Still,
cobwebby Oscar scared me. Carl, huge in death as well,
beckoned

from the Fibber McGhee closet where his yellowed tennis
rackets, screwed into cases,
stood, perpetually unused.
In drawers in the chest on the sun porch lay his office memos,
some grainy photographs, one of Carl, pipe in hand, in a rocking
chair, inscrutable.

My grandmother never uttered his name.
Perhaps she'd had all of Carl she needed.

From the creased photo, my mother at sixteen,
smiles, my father—absent since I was an infant—
behind her, hands clasped around her waist, pipe jutting
over her shoulder, handsome, magnanimous
but knowable only from this photo,
taxidermied himself.

Usage

I don't remember the book or context where the word
appeared.
But the faded brocade couch where I read smelled of
cedar and dust
and the stretch from the living room to the kitchen where
the women were
was long, like the pall of silence
that followed my yelling, "What is castrate?"

My great aunt delivered the definition
to my mortification
a year before my uncle, who had secretly
followed me to the cellar,
stood smiling at the top of the stairs,

years before I could apply the definition.

Roar

for A.V.

Every April when the explosions
of forsythia occur, I recall the blast
of my landlord's chainsaw, how

without any warning
he hacked down to nubs
the forsythia that lit my deck.

I wept from the shock of it,
for the bell blossoms executed
for the leaves deprived of their nascence,

for my own helplessness.
April 7th cancer took your life
but I keep hearing your laugh

exploding in the dark
of the movie theater.
Singular and irrepressible,

it landed on the ears of the staid viewers
like an insult,
like your vow to vitality.

Loud Family

From my beach towel dugout
I eavesdrop on the people
nearby, trying to forget
the loud family who arrived
at midnight
at the room adjoining mine.
Cranky now because the Cape May beach
is filling up, I walk down to the shore
where the waves repeat themselves
and the sudden arcs of those dolphins
beckon all of us in.

A Ghost Speaks Down to Earthly About Visitations

We return to oblige the living
who simply wish to have us back
or to make peace with us.
We have our own amends to make
but as ghosts aren't our wrongs against you
rendered moot? By virtue of our ghostliness?
Isn't it too late to settle earthly business?
All wrongs against each other,
all animal and natural debts
go now to vapor.

Acknowledgements

I gratefully acknowledge the following publications in which some of these poems first appeared:

The American Poetry Review: "One Summer"
The Drunken Boat (online): "A Winter Reunion"
Spillway: "Ideal Woman"
Mad Poets Review: "Those Cows at 'The Roost'"
A Moonstone Chapbook *From the Familiar:* The Moonstone Press
Hubbub: "Blood Moon"

Many thanks to Nick Courtright and Atmosphere Press for publishing this manuscript; many thanks to my editor Kyle McCord for his help with reordering it.

Heartfelt thanks to Cathy Cohen and Alyson Adler, for their workshop support and abiding friendship; to Nathalie Anderson and Eleanor Wilner, for their coaching, confidence and abiding friendship; to my family for their abiding love, support and faith in my poems.

About Atmosphere Press

Atmosphere Press is an independent, full-service publisher for excellent books in all genres and for all audiences. Learn more about what we do at atmospherepress.com.

We encourage you to check out some of Atmosphere's latest releases, which are available at Amazon.com and via order from your local bookstore:

In the Cloakroom of Proper Musings, a lyric narrative by Kristina Moriconi

Lucid_Malware.zip, poetry by Dylan Sonderman

The Unordering of Days, poetry by Jessica Palmer

It's Not About You, poetry by Daniel Casey

A Dream of Wide Water, poetry by Sharon Whitehill

Radical Dances of the Ferocious Kind, poetry by Tina Tru

The Woods Hold Us, poetry by Makani Speier-Brito

My Cemetery Friends: A Garden of Encounters at Mount Saint Mary in Queens, New York, nonfiction and poetry by Vincent J. Tomeo

Report from the Sea of Moisture, poetry by Stuart Jay Silverman

The Enemy of Everything, poetry by Michael Jones

The Stargazers, poetry by James McKee

The Pretend Life, poetry by Michelle Brooks

Minnesota and Other Poems, poetry by Daniel N. Nelson

Interviews from the Last Days, sci-fi poetry by Christina Loraine

About the Author

Katherine Barham received an MFA from Warren Wilson Program for Writers and her poems have appeared in *The American Poetry Review, The Drunken Boat, Spillway, Mad Poets Review, Hubbub, North of Oxford* (January, 2021). Katherine's chapbook, *From the Familiar,* was published by Moonstone Press in 2015. Katherine is a retired high school English teacher and  currently resides in Rose Valley, PA, birdwatching with her cat Elliott.